Children don't divorce

Rosemary Stones

Illustrated by Nicola Spoor

Happy Cat Books

When me and my brother were little
there was a lot of fun in our house.
My dad would tease me
and we would all play games together.
Mum and Dad would hold hands and hug each other.

When I was six and Peter was four, it changed.
There wasn't any laughing any more.
Dad was out all the time.
I'd come downstairs and find Mum crying.
She'd say, "Oh, I'm just tired"
but I knew it was more than that.

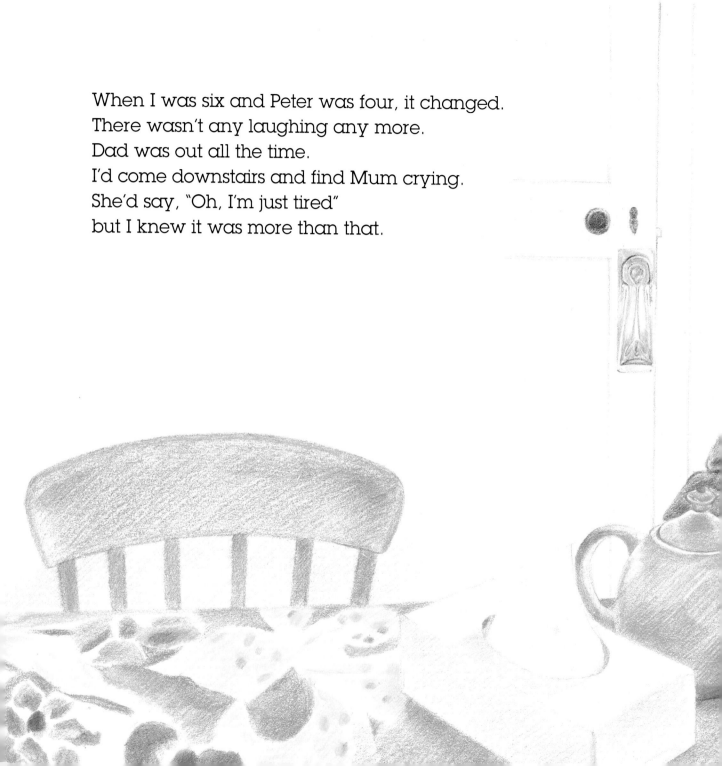

One night I suddenly woke up.
Mum and Dad were shouting and fighting.
I heard things falling on the floor.
Peter woke up too and we both started to cry.

After that Mum and Dad hardly spoke to each other.
It was horrible. I'd ask Dad if I could go to the park
and he'd say "Ask your mother".
I'd ask Mum for money for the school trip
and she'd say "Ask your father".

It was hard at school. I was thinking about
Mum and Dad and I couldn't pay attention.
My teacher asked what the matter was
but I didn't know what to say.
I just said "Nothing".

One day Dad just didn't come home.
He'd taken all his clothes and his records.
Mum said he'd left us.
It was a shock but somehow I wasn't surprised.
I'd known something was going to happen.
Mum said she and Dad were going to divorce.

I felt very scared. I had bad dreams.
I'd get up in the middle of the night
and get into Mum's bed where Dad used to sleep.
Peter started wetting the bed again
even though he was a big boy of four.
He was always whining and crying.

One day at school Gavin in my class
teased me about my picture.
I just went mad and started hitting him.
Miss had to stop me. Afterwards she was nice.
She said she knew about Dad going
and I could talk to her about it whenever I wanted.

I wanted Mum to explain why she and Dad
were going to divorce.
She said that they didn't get on any more
but they still loved me and Peter.

Whenever Mum started crying, I'd say
"Why don't you and Dad get together again
and we'll be a family like before?"
Mum said it wouldn't work.

I didn't know what to tell my friends
about Dad going. I didn't say anything.
When they asked me where my dad was
I said he'd gone away for work.
Then Imogen in my class said her dad
didn't live at home with her and her mum.
He'd left when she was two.
Rosa said she lived with just her dad.
I was surprised that there were other children
whose parents didn't live together any more.

I thought that Dad might have left because
me and Peter had done something wrong.
Imogen and Rosa said it had nothing to do with the children
but with the mums and dads.

Mum and Dad couldn't agree
about who should look after us.
Mum said that Dad had gone to live with Stella
and it wasn't right for him to have us.
I didn't know what to say.
I wanted my dad as well as my mum.
It wasn't fair when other children have
their dad every day.

When Dad came to visit us, Peter would talk
like a baby and cry when Dad had to go.
I felt so sad, as though I was being split in two.

A court welfare officer came to talk to me.
She was friendly. She asked about school
and I told her about the swimming gala.
I said I loved my mum and I loved my dad
and so did Peter.

Now that it's sorted out, Peter and me
live with Mum and go to see Dad at weekends.
I can't have a cuddle with Dad every day any more
but it's all right. He talks to me a lot
and he's teaching me to ride my bike and write poems.

At first I didn't like to see him with Stella.
It didn't seem right. He should have been home with Mum.
I still find it strange that Dad's not at home.
Half of me seems to go one way and half the other.

After Dad went, Mum cried a lot and she was lonely.
Now she's much happier.
Peter and me went to see where she works
and we had tea in the office canteen!

Mum has a boyfriend now. She met him at work.
His name is Brian. At first I didn't like him.
I was afraid Mum wouldn't love me
and Peter any more. Also it made me realise
that Dad and Mum won't get back together again ever.

Now I'm glad Mum is happy with Brian.
I think he's nice. He doesn't pretend he's my dad.
He says he's a Step-Brian.

Once I thought Peter and me were the only children
in the world whose parents were divorced.
Now I know there are lots of children like us.
It's OK to love your mum and love your dad.
Even if they don't want to live with each other,
they are still your parents.

Now I know that when my parents divorced,
it wasn't because of me and Peter.
Parents can divorce but not children.
Even if they don't live together, your mum and dad
will always be your mum and dad.